Two of a Kind

D1593118

Two of a Kind

Dogs that Look Like Their Owners

Photographs by
Larry Bercow

Text by
Zachary Schisgal

WARNER BOOKS

A Time Warner Company

Warner Books, Inc., 1271 Avenue of the Americas, New York, NY 10020
Visit our Web site at www.warnerbooks.com

 A Time Warner Company

Printed in the United States of America

First Printing: July 1999

10 9 8 7 6 5 4 3 2 1

Library of Congress Cataloging-in-Publication Data

Bercow, Larry
    Two of a kind : dogs that look like their owners / photographs by
Larry Bercow , text by Zachary Schisgal.
        p.   cm.
    ISBN 0-446-67479-6
    1. Dogs—Pictorial works.   2. Dog owners—Pictorial works.
I. Schisgal, Zachary.   II. Title.
SF430.B46   1999   99-11793
779' .2—dc21   CIP

Book design and text composition by H. Roberts Design
Cover design by Carolyn Lechter
Cover photograph by Larry Bercow

ATTENTION: SCHOOLS AND CORPORATIONS
WARNER books are available at quantity discounts with bulk purchase for educational, business, or sales promotional use. For information, please write to: SPECIAL SALES DEPARTMENT, WARNER BOOKS, 1271 AVENUE OF THE AMERICAS, NEW YORK, N.Y. 10020

Acknowledgments

*T*he authors would like to thank the countless dog owners and dog lovers who lent their time and insight to this project. We hope that this tribute to the relationship of dog and owner does justice to the wonderful human-canine relationships we discovered along the way.

In addition, thanks to Klaudia Bercow for her generous help. And to Elizabeth Niles for her continued support. Thanks to Jennifer Hengen for her energetic representation, and our editor at Warner Books, Amy Einhorn, whose enthusiasm, talent, and hard work helped make this possible.

Introduction

Who hasn't walked down the street and remarked on how much a dog and its owner look alike? Perhaps it was the hair color, a facial feature like eyes, or even, sometimes, girth. Does the owner realize these similarities exist?

Two of a Kind shows what we've all noticed in our neighborhoods, or maybe even in ourselves—that owners and their dogs truly do look alike. Whether it's the shape of the ears or nose, color of the eyes or hair and coat, many owners bare an uncanny resemblance to the dogs that share their lives. But as we took these photographs and looked at them later, we noticed a different kind of resemblance as well. Sometimes an owner and her dog are looking back with the same facial expression, or they will hold their head at the same angle. Other times, their eyes seem to be saying the same thing. In a sequence of photographs, owner and dog constantly change expression, but in each photograph, they have the same expression as each other. The owner and his dog shared a disposition—an outlook on life and on the moment—as well as a look.

Setting out to photograph people who look like their dogs promised to be a daunting task. Approach strangers on the street—on the streets of New York, no less—and tell them they look like their canine companion? Of course, the reality turned out to be the exact opposite of what we expected. Many owners were downright flattered, and it became clear to us that dogs were like surrogate children to the owners. Well, that must explain the physical similarities. Owners cooked for their dogs, talked to their dogs constantly, and boasted about their accomplishments.

We met a wide range of wonderful people putting this book together—and encountered a wide range of opinions. Some owners had heard that they resembled their dogs, some seemed to play it up a bit, but others were surprised when we approached them. While owners may have adopted a dog that resembled them, or adopted a look to match their dog, it appeared that something else was at work. For most owners, their dog is a soul mate, a true source of joy in their life. The words "love," "fun," and "affection" kept coming up. Whether owners found their dogs with breeders or at the pound, the dog was an equal in the relationship—if not, we sensed sometimes, the one who called the shots. There was many a cold, wet winter day we spent with owners who patiently sat and talked in a dog run, giving their dogs a chance to get out and play. In return, the dogs were always looking to their owners for an "okay," a subtle nod that the owner had an eye on them. As much as was spoken between owner and dog, we also found something that was unspoken and meaningful.

Two of a Kind tries to capture both relationships: the intriguing physical similarities that we notice between owner and dog and the less obvious but ever-present bond that unites them. These ties can be seen in the following photographs as owner and dog prove they are, indeed, two of a kind.

Two of a Kind

Margot and Miloche

Margot was drawn to Miloche's eyes when they first met two and a half years ago. Miloche loves to eat fruit, especially papaya, passion fruit, and mango. Margot and Miloche take a step class together, which keeps them fit for walks in the park.

Central Park, New York
October 18, 1997

2

Gregory and Piglet

Riverside Park, New York
March 9, 1998

Jackie and
Isadora Penelope Goldberg

West End Avenue, New York
May 4, 1997

Helen and Harry

Riverside Park, New York
August 25, 1997

Nancy and Sally

Riverside Park, New York
May 4, 1997

Paula and Zevon

Paula describes Zevon as a thirty-pound chicken with an eighty-pound bark. But she also thinks he's the cutest dog in the world.

Cark Schurz Park, New York
November 22, 1997

Pam and Federico Fellini

Pam likes to take Federico walking on Mulberry Street in New York's Little Italy every night, where the neighborhood fans yell, "Ciao Fellini!" Fellini, who ate biscotti while we photographed him, is a real Italian love dog.

Little Italy, New York
May 2, 1998

Peter and Sophie

Sophie, who used to fall asleep in Peter's arms as a puppy, is a "sweetheart, big cream puff."

Central Park, New York
May 29, 1998

Katharina and Sky

According to Katharina, a professional photographer, Sky likes to sit in front of the camera when Katharina is taking pictures. So Katharina and Sky were both great subjects when we photographed them.

Madison Square Park, New York
December 16, 1998

John and Kahuna

In a house full of animals, Kahuna competes to be top dog with Abby, a Cockatoo that likes to bark.

Riverside Park, New York
May 4, 1997

Elizabeth and Becca

Elizabeth and Becca have modeled together before—for drawing classes in Soho.

Soho, New York
June 4, 1997

Robert and Wolfgang

Wolfgang is one of the best shoppers in Soho. When Robert and Wolfgang go shopping together, Wolfgang will bark when Robert tries something on he doesn't like.

Soho, New York
January 16, 1998

Deborah and Henry

Deborah calls her five years with Henry the best in her life.

Central Park, New York
October 18, 1997

Kurt and Barli

Barli, a Wheaten Terrier, doesn't love poodles, but he does love his owner, Kurt. Even though Barli is incredibly affectionate, Kurt complains that Barli doesn't listen to a word he says. Together, they enjoy life in Manhattan and Aspen.

Central Park, New York
October 18, 1998

Julia and Buddy

Julia had ten cats and a dog, but made room for Buddy when she found him wandering the streets of Astoria, Queens.

Central Park, New York
October 18, 1997

Monica and George

Central Park, New York
October 18, 1998

Judy and Daffodil

Columbus Avenue, New York
January 4, 1998

George and Stella

Stella weighs 170 pounds. Together, George and Stella take walks in Tompkins Square Park.

Tompkins Square Park, New York
November 15, 1997

Terri and Déjà Vu Monster Mash

Have we seen these two before?

Madison Square Garden
February 16, 1998

Seth and Angus

Tompkins Square Park, New York
November 15, 1997

Dee and Jazz

Jazz loves to walk in the park. Dee loves Jazz music and, of course, her Cocker Spaniel, Jazz.

Riverside Park, New York
May 3, 1998

Yuri and Sharik

East Village, New York
March 7, 1998

Robert and Burroughs

Robert found Burroughs in the borough of Brooklyn, New York.

Tompkins Square Park, New York
April 4, 1998

Nick and Video Vixen

Nick promised to name his dog after a movie title in his friend's video rental store—Nick picked "Video Vixen." We guess this is better than taking "I Know What You Did Last Summer" for a walk in the park.

Riverside Park, New York
May 4, 1997

Stephanie and Minimus

Only six months old, and Minimus is already up to
Stephanie's shin.

Madison Square Park, New York
December 6, 1997

Claude, Monique, and Gracy

Claude, Monique, and Gracy on Prince Street in Soho.

Soho, New York
March 22, 1998

Van and Pepis

Van's girlfriend wanted to name this German Shepherd Pepsi, but he misunderstood.

Tompkins Square Park, New York
April 4, 1998

Alyce and Liz

Liz is an accomplished model—maybe you've seen her on a greeting card. And, yes, on the card she's wearing an afghan.

Washington Square Park, New York
January 18, 1998

Katherine and Blackjack

Blackjack, three years old, likes chewing bubble gum, which makes the streets of New York a treasure trove.

Washington Square Park, New York
January 18, 1998

Reina and Beccy

Reina calls Beccy a "pound treasure." We agree.

Stuyvesant Square, New York
February 9, 1998

Paul, Betty Lynn, and Daisy Mae

Paul says that Betty Lynn and Daisy Mae are "both perfectly well brought up young ladies." But we have a hard time telling these sisters apart.

Riverside Park, New York
March 9, 1998

Patricia and Fanny

Greenwich Village, New York
February 8, 1998

Delphine and Mookie

Mookie, named after a favorite New York Met player Mookie Wilson, likes to take peanuts out of the shell and eat them.

Tompkins Square Park, New York
April 4, 1998

Alex and Luigi

Tompkins Square Park, New York
January 24, 1998

Don, Chase, and Taylor

Riverside Park, New York
May 3, 1998

Jeff and Hubert

Fifth Avenue, New York
April 12, 1998

Lucinda and Sasha

Lucinda says that Sasha, who's seventeen years old, has mellowed with age. They're at a Dachshund convention in Washington Square Park.

Washington Square Park, New York
April 25, 1998

Kyoko and Atom

Riverside Park, New York
May 3, 1998

Joseph and Tyra

Joseph says that Tyra, part Stafffordshire Terrier, is lovable.

Riverside Park, New York
May 3, 1998

Ali and Barkley

Riverside Park, New York
December 21, 1997

Bonnie and Shana

Washington Square Park, New York
April 25, 1998

Craig and Chaos

Riverside Park, New York
May 3, 1998

Eugene and Jazz

Eugene admired Jazz's tuxedo when he found the young puppy.

Little Italy, New York
May 24, 1998

Place a photograph of you and your dog here.